"Carol Pack and Barbara Paskoff's Our Coronavirus Diary does a surprisingly good job of taking potshots at a pandemic the likes of which no one presently alive has ever experienced before. The cartoons are right on point and often hilarious, and the diary entries will appeal to anyone who's experienced the dubious pleasures of sheltering in place day after day after day.

Most highly recommended."
       — Jack Magnus for Readers' Favorite

Our Coronavirus Diary

Another brain-fart from Over-Sixty: Shades of Gray

Artiqua Press

PACK & PASKOFF

No part of this publication may be reproduced, distributed or transmitted in any form or by any means, including photocopying, recording, or other electronic, digital or mechanical methods without the prior written permission of the publisher, except in the case of brief quotations embodied in critical reviews and certain other noncommercial uses permitted by copyright law. For permission requests, contact the publisher with "Attention: Permissions Coordinator" in the subject line.

ARTIQUA PRESS
www.artiquapress.com
info@artiquapress.com
Westbury, NY 11590

TRADE PAPERBACK

August 25, 2020

OUR CORONAVIRUS DIARY
Copyright © 2020 Carol Pack & Barbara Paskoff
All rights reserved.

ISBN-13: 978-1-970028-07-2

A message from those crazy old broads at
"Over-Sixty: Shades of Gray"

Dear Reader,

Like most people, we've never experienced a pandemic that has shut down our country and made us fear for our future, our friends, and our families — both health-wise and economically.

COVID-19 is serious stuff. It's devastating. And our hearts go out to everyone who has suffered through it or lost someone to it. It is not our intention that anything published in this book diminishes that loss.

That said, it is our belief that life with all its treacherous dips and turns is easier to take with a spoonful of sugar. We like to look for the humor in everything because we believe it knocks the things that scare us down to size, making us feel more in control, so we can deal with our fears more easily.

We apologize if you're offended, hurt, or think us entirely inappropriate for the content in "Our Coronavirus Diary," or OCD for short. We are what we are, over-sixty and still going strong. Well, maybe not strong, but at least we're still going.

Thank God for adult diapers.

Sincerely,

Carol & Barbara

Or as we like to refer to ourselves,
Yin & Yang (and yes, she's still yanging my yin)

2020

SUN	MON	TUE	WED	THU	FRI	SAT
	01	02	02	03	04	05
06	07	08	09	10	11	12
13	14	15	16	17	18	19
20	21	22	23	24	25	26
27	28	29	30			

Coronavirus Lockdown – Day 1

Dear Diary,

This crazy virus has everyone going nuts. Not us. We're pretty level-headed and it will all be over before we know it. Fingers crossed.

"There's nothing to worry about regarding this national emergency."

PANDEMIC JEOPARDY

MISTAKES WERE MADE	TIGER KING	QUARANTINED CELEBRITIES	HOARDING	SEPARATE STAYCATIONS	THINGS NOT CANCELLED
$200	$200	$200	$200	$200	$200
$400	$400	$400	$400	$400	$400
$600	$600	$600	$600	$600	$600
$800	$800	$800	$800	$800	$800
$1000	$1000	$1000	$1000	$1000	$1000

bob

Coronavirus Lockdown — Day 4

Dear Diary,

This isn't so bad. We were already retired, and being in lockdown is just like that. Boring. But it gives us plenty of time to binge-watch all our favorite TV shows.

Coronavirus Lockdown — Day 7

Dear Diary,

What's all the hubbub about toilet paper? We heard people are hoarding it and store shelves are empty. Does coronavirus make people poop more? That's a silver lining. Goodness knows, sitting around all day eating snack foods can be constipating.

Coronavirus Lockdown – Day 10

Dear Diary,

Well, I'm not dead yet, but that doesn't mean I haven't stopped thinking about my death tenfold since the news of the coronavirus broke.

Prior to the shit hitting the fan, I was in the hospital with pneumonia. I was in one day and out the next. My nurses and doctors said, "Go home, it's worse here. Lots of sickness." Who knew what they were talking about? Certainly not I. The coronavirus wasn't on my radar screen. But when I got home it was the only thing on my television screen.

I checked all the boxes for "You're in deep shit." It was like filling out a profile for Match.com. Age — I am over seventy. Health — I have underlying conditions. All around physicality — my immune system is shot to hell.

The only thing I have to look forward to is a bagel and cream cheese. Which, by the way, I would never consider eating prior because it was too fattening. Not a problem now. I'm sure the coffin will fit.

I feel incredibly vulnerable. Scared for my life, or what's left of it.

If the virus should take mine, I've put together a "Kick the Bucket" list for the undertaker, with sample sizes of all my favorite makeup, a wig already styled, and my favorite red leather skirt from my youth. Sure, it's a size two, but if they have to cut it up the back to make it fit, who's gonna know? Besides, it will give the folks at the pearly gates a free show!

Coronavirus Lockdown — Day 13

Dear Diary,

Do we need masks? Don't we need masks? We're getting conflicting information. Still, it wouldn't hurt to buy some if we could find any. They have plenty of other advantages, and will come in especially handy if we run out of toilet paper.

Coronavirus Lockdown – Day 16

Coronavirus Lockdown — Day 19

Dear Diary,

I should have been a hoarder! Have you tried to book delivery service with a grocery store? Getting a date is like winning the lottery. And even when you do, you're not guaranteed to get what you asked for. Have egg-laying chickens gone on strike? And where are my Bubba Burgers?

"How was panic shopping?"

Shopping List

Eggs
X OUT OF STOCK

Milk
X OUT OF STOCK

Bread
X OUT OF STOCK

Bubba Burgers
X OUT OF STOCK

Toilet Paper
X OUT OF STOCK

Paper Towels
X OUT OF STOCK

Hand Sanitizer
X OUT OF STOCK

Disinfectant Spray
X OUT OF STOCK

Antiseptic Wipes
X OUT OF STOCK

Sanity
X OUT OF MY MIND

Coronavirus Lockdown – Day 22

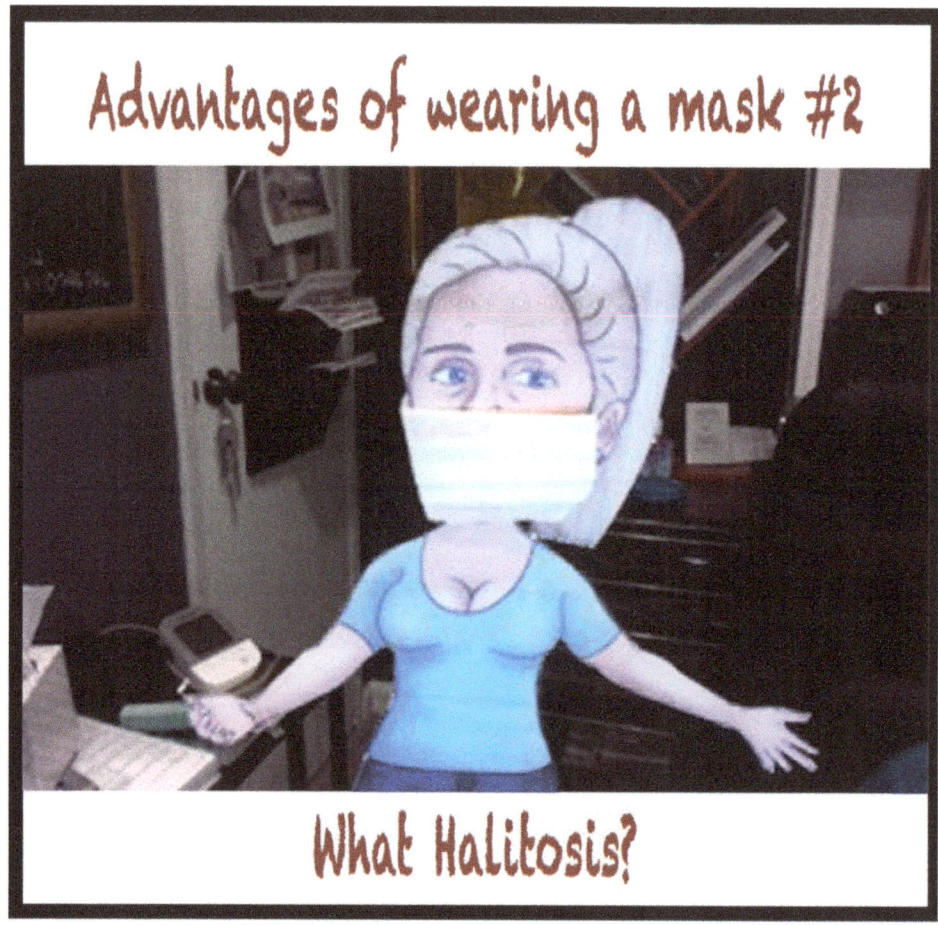

Our Coronavirus Diary

Coronavirus Lockdown — Day 25

Dear Diary,

What's the deal with social distancing? Someone said six-feet, but that's how deep they dig graves, so we don't like that one. Eight-feet is OK, as long as we're not stuck walking in the middle of the street. Not that there are a lot of cars with everyone isolated inside, but the few there are ALL speed — because they can. Besides, if the coronavirus can travel thirteen feet, what good is eight-foot social distancing?

Coronavirus Lockdown — Day 28

Dear Diary,

It's been a month since everything shut down, but they keep moving the finish line. I thought this would be OK for a week or two, but things are getting tight. Like my pants. It seems like COVID-19 stands for how many pounds we've gained since starting isolation. We need to open the malls again, if only to buy pants with elastic waistbands.

"I'm just saying, when this pandemic ends I can't go out until I lose ten pounds."

Coronavirus Lockdown – Day 31

I wanted to use the lockdown productively, I learned cosmetic surgery.

Coronavirus Lockdown – Day 34

Dear Diary,

Living in fear of the coronavirus is so aging. My jowls look jowlier. My laugh lines aren't funny. And Jell-O isn't the only thing I watch "jiggle." However, nonessential medical services are now off the table, and my plastic surgeon has gone to the Hamptons to self-isolate. Still, I'm sure I can find do-it-yourself tips on YouTube.

Coronavirus Lockdown — Day 37

Dear Diary,

We don't even want to watch the news anymore. Every day, there's something new to worry about. At least there's drama at the daily White House briefings when the president calls a reporter "terrible" for asking a "nasty question." Then there's dissension between POTUS and his health officials who sometimes cringe on-camera when the leader of the free world says something stupid. Too bad the news is the most entertaining show on TV right now. A word of advice: bleach does not belong inside your body.

"I find wearing a mask helps."

Coronavirus Lockdown – Day 40

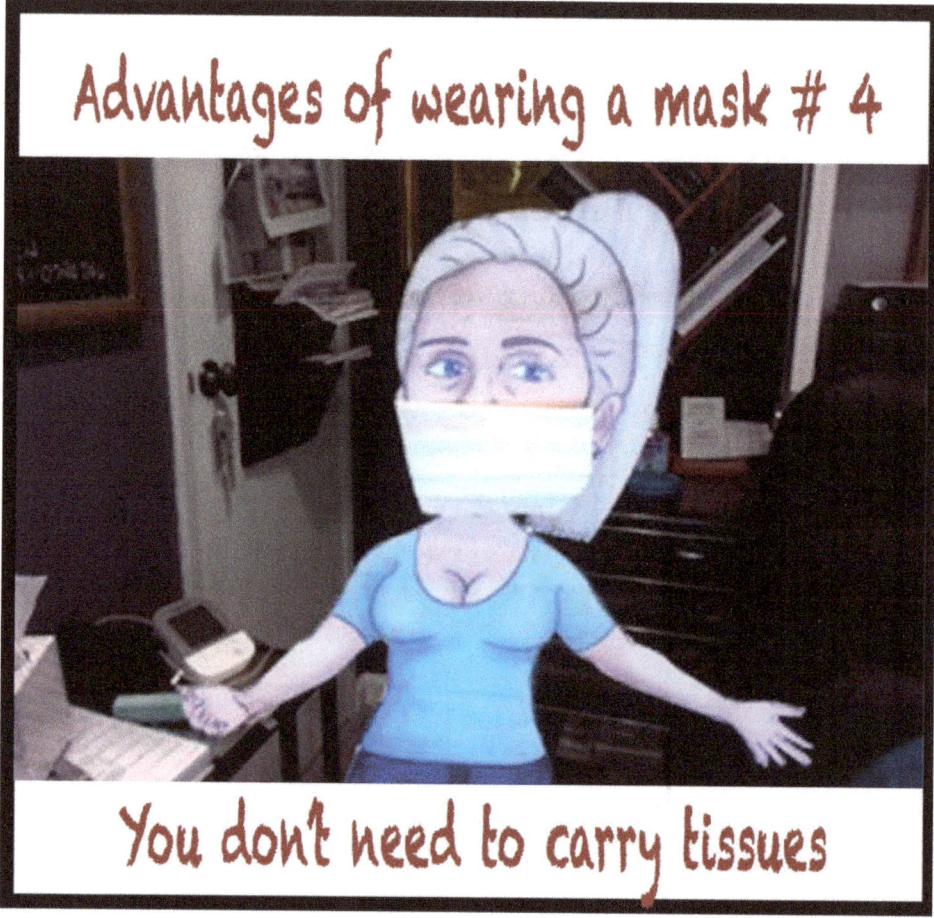

Coronavirus Lockdown — Day 43

Dear Diary,

Lysol Disinfectant Spray? Hand sanitizer? Clorox wipes? My kingdom for a bottle of Purell!

It's like WWII rations all over again. From now on, everyone only gets three squares a day.

Of toilet paper.

Coronavirus Lockdown — Day 46

Dear Diary,

Sometimes, you've got to think outside the box when it comes to dealing with the pandemic. And often, we can find the answer using common everyday household items.

Improvisation can be so freeing.

Coronavirus Lockdown — Day 49

Coronavirus Lockdown — Day 52

Dear Diary,

The roller-coaster effect of the coronavirus on the stock market is going to give me a heart attack. It's up. It's down. It's up. It's down. So, it's actually the virus that's giving me an underlying condition. I just can't win.

"So, I'm going to live but my stocks are on life support?"

Coronavirus Lockdown — Day 55

Dear Diary,

Social distancing guidelines prevent us from embracing all the essential people, working the frontlines, however, each and every one of them deserves a hug along with our undying gratitude. The key word here is, "undying."

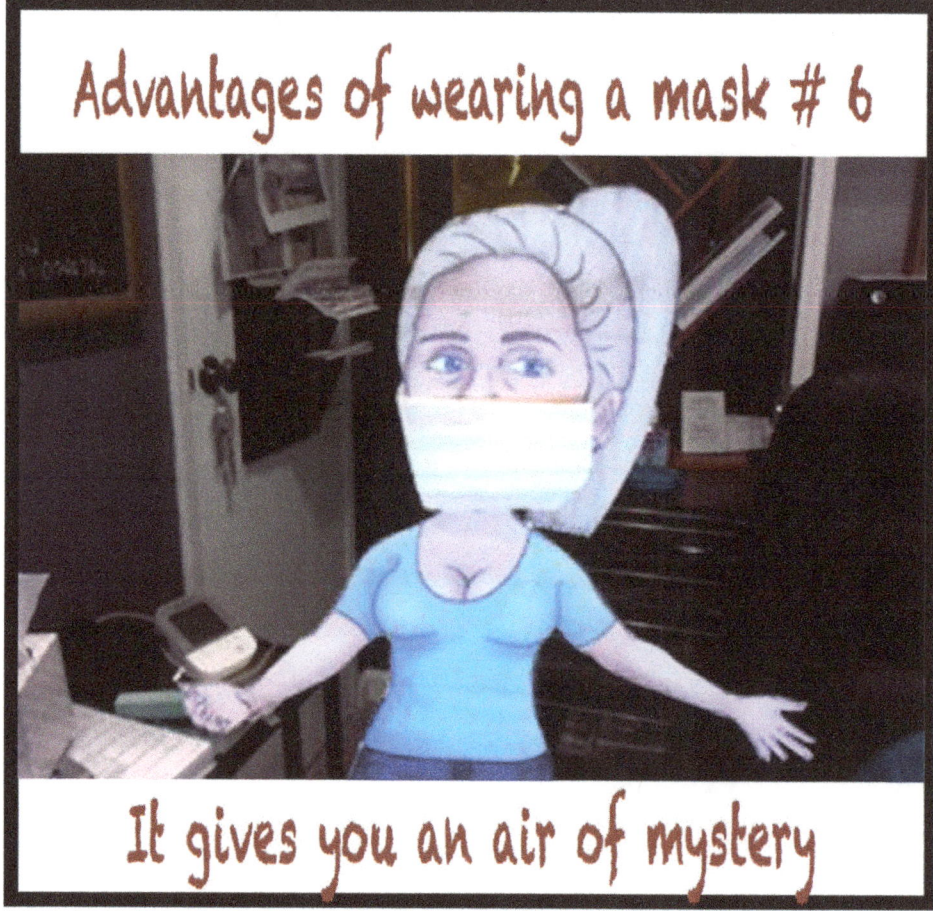

Desperate times call for desperate measures.

Coronavirus Lockdown — Day 61

Dear Diary,

With so many shortages in the stores and erratic delivery, we have had to learn to improvise.

Did you know they actually have these washable squares that you can use in place of tissues?

They're called handkerchiefs!

Coronavirus Lockdown — Day 64

Dear Diary,

I feel relieved. I feel less guilty. My vagina is free. It has been emancipated. And all it took was the coronavirus to avoid unwanted company.

I can throw away my list: "Ways to Avoid Sex." I'm now healthy. No more yeast infections. No more UTIs. No more headaches. No more backaches or "I'm too tired."

As long as his penis follows social distancing, I'm good!

Give that man a hand — preferably his own.

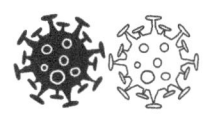

Coronavirus Lockdown — Day 67

Dear Diary,

I feel so alone. I tried to keep a con man on the phone today after he demanded a gift card for an amount he says I "owe" the IRS. But before I finished complaining about my bunions and the lack of nonessential medical services, he had the nerve to hang up on me!

Coronavirus Lockdown – Day 70

Coronavirus Lockdown — Day 73

Dear Diary,

I never knew what cabin fever was because I don't own a cabin. And then we went into lockdown. It makes people a little nutty, and like coronavirus, nuts could be hazardous to your health.

Potus position

Coronavirus Lockdown — Day 76

Dear Diary,

They say exercise will keep us sane. We've been adapting our yoga poses, to reflect our current attitude.

"Om" my!

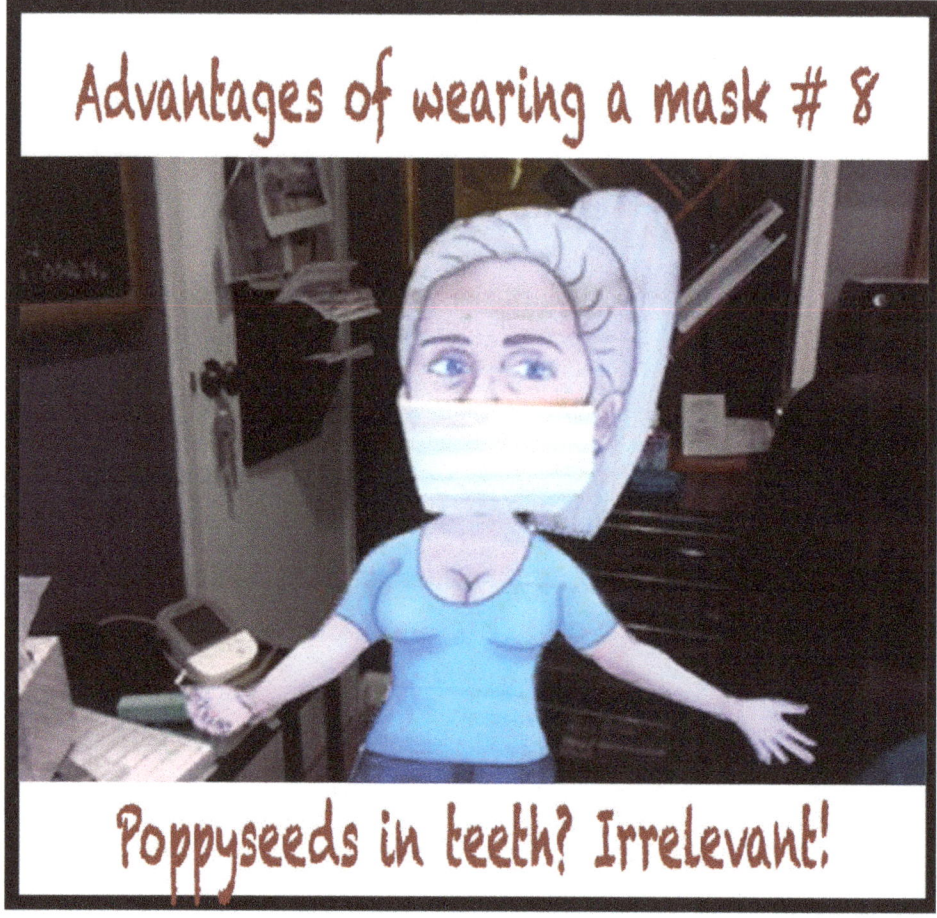

Coronavirus Lockdown – Day 82

Dear Diary,

I want to go to a beach. Or a baseball game. Or a concert. How bad can it be? Still, if I end up positive for coronavirus, don't send me to the hospital. Or a nursing home. Just let me expire at home – like all the library books under my bed.

"Sorry – there's a shortage of beds. On the bright side, you're way more infectious than the guy next to you."

Coronavirus Lockdown - Day 85

Dear Diary,

My fingernails are little nubs. My feet are calloused and swollen with toenails like lethal spears. And my hair? Let's not even go there. I had to cover all my mirrors. Whose big idea was it to deem hairstylists and manicurists nonessential? It's their fault I'm having an existential breakdown!

Coronavirus Lockdown - Day 88

Dear Diary,

It sucks being old, especially when we're in the demographic that's the center of the COVID-19 bulls-eye. It's not bad enough we have a new pain every day and our bowels are acting up. Now we have to wonder if the delivery guy with our fajitas is asymptomatic, and nobody realizes that sneaky COVID-19 virus is oozing from his pores!

Coronavirus Lockdown – Day 91

Dear Diary,

Ohmygod, ohmygod, ohmygod, I touched my face. It was right after I received a shipment of toilet paper, but before I disinfected it. I sneezed and automatically covered my face with my hands. Now I may have coronavirus germs crawling all over me while my hands are full of sneezy-snot.

Why me?

Coronavirus Lockdown – Day 94

"What wine goes best with vodka?"

Coronavirus Lockdown - Day 97

Dear Diary,

Drink.

Eat.

Drink.

Eat.

Drink.

Eat.

Drink.

Eat!

I gained so much weight, that when I got into my bed last night, that was tight!

Never in my lifetime did I ever think we would be going through this nightmare. It's so scary. So, I'm finding my comfort in eating and drinking. And I will continue to get fat and stay buzzed until I understand what this "new normal" is that everyone is talking about.

And if we ever do see the light of day, my first two trips will be to Alcoholics and Overeaters Anonymous.

Passing out! Again.

And again.

And again.

Coronavirus Lockdown – Day 100

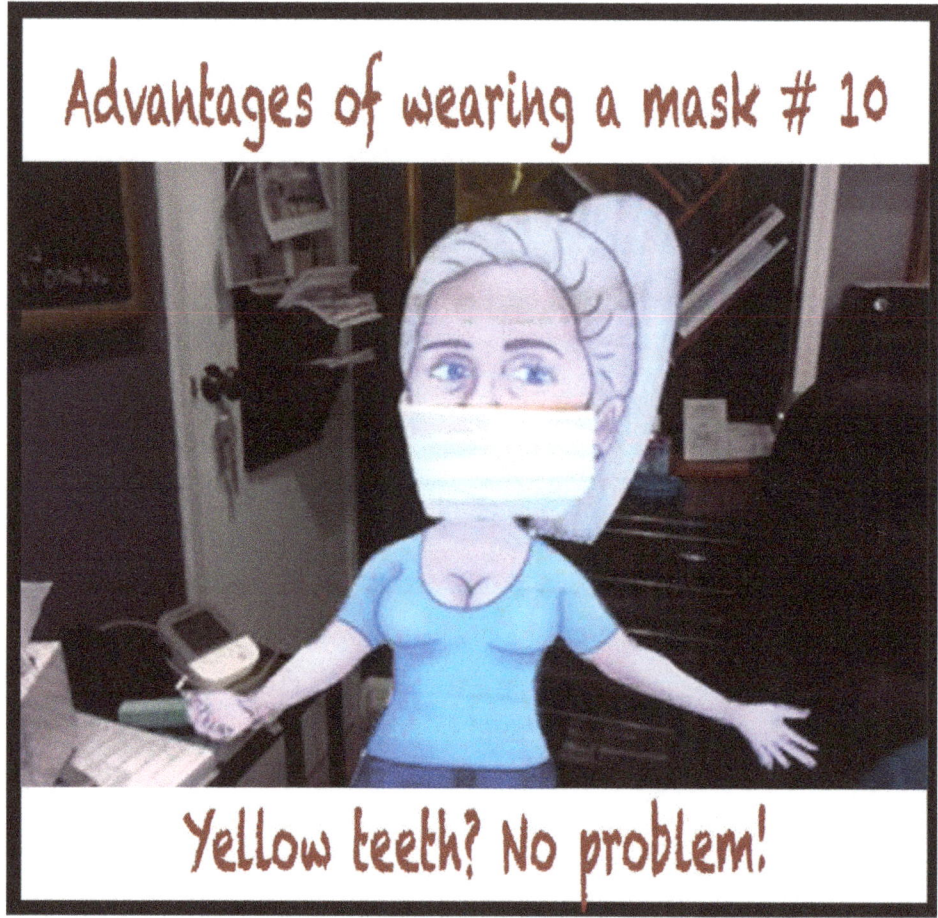

Coronavirus Lockdown - Day 103

"How much longer with this social distancing thing?"

"Considering our advanced age, we'll probably forget to care long before we have to stop."

"Think it can last 20 seconds this time?"

Coronavirus Lockdown – Day 106

Dear Diary,

If what they say is true, that "cleanliness is next to godliness," well, then I'm a fucking saint!

And just when I thought my hypochondria was subsiding, along comes the coronavirus.

Unfortunately, my anxieties most always manifest themselves as physical symptoms. So, to say I'm paranoid about handwashing, about wiping down packages, about washing produce, is right on point – twice a day I sterilize doorknobs, telephones, computers, etc. I'm going crazy. And if I think my clothing touched a contaminant, I wash it. I'm so exhausted.

I've had sore throats I thought were COVID-19, a cold I thought was COVID-19, headaches, body aches, and blurry vision. Believe me there is more, but I'm running out of paper.

I feel so vulnerable, so out of control and crazy. OH MY GOD, I CAN'T STAND ME!

I have hunkered down in my house for more than ninety days before going out into my own backyard. I have kept my husband prisoner because he has underlying conditions and is a senior. And if you think that was easy… OY!

However, I've ordered a new gadget that's sure to make life more convenient and bug the bug. As soon as anyone walks through my door, they'll be bathed in ultraviolet light, sprayed with Lysol from a dozen different nozzles, and a choir will sing a medley of the "Hallelujah Chorus," "Happy Trails," and "So Long, Farewell" by the von Trapp Family Singers.

Coronavirus Lockdown – Day 109

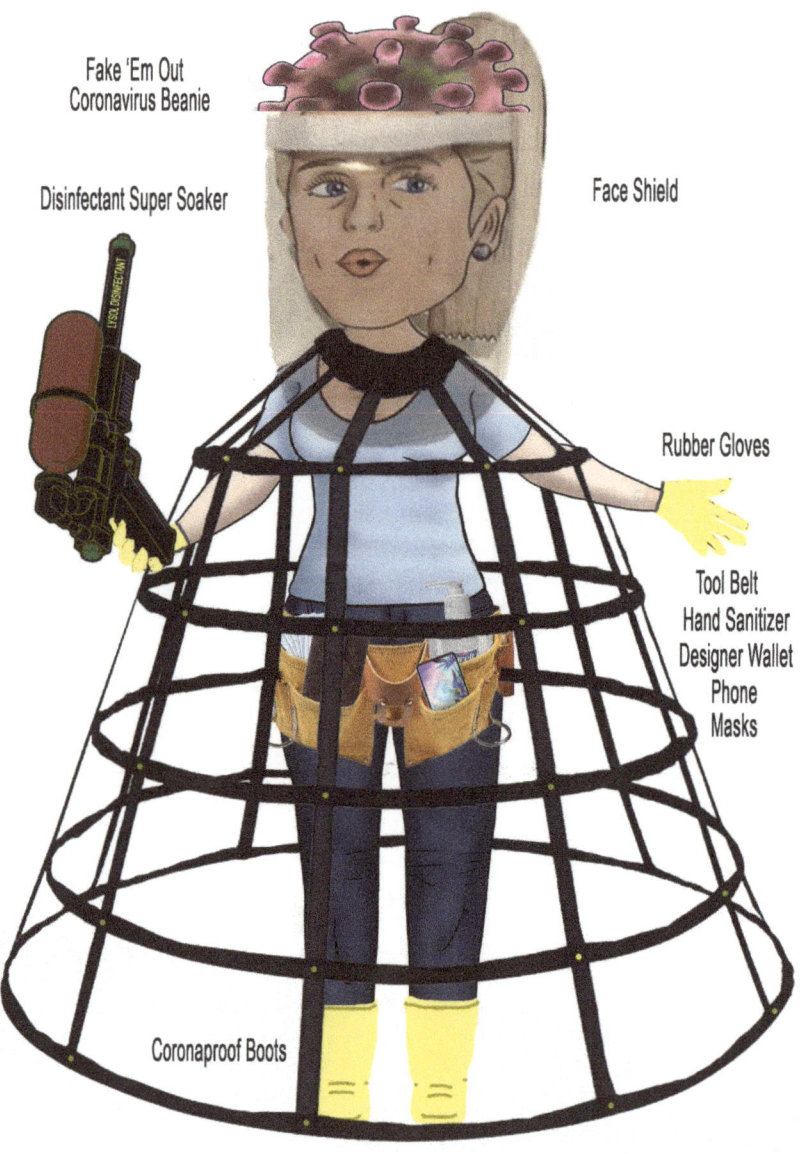

Dressed to Kill (coronavirus droplets)

Coronavirus Lockdown - Day 112

Coronavirus Lockdown – Phase Out 1

Dear Diary,

We're feeling a little seasick with all the talk of second waves and spikes. Although, maybe it's us because we're "quaking" in our boots. A lot of places have reopened for business. It's good if they're making more toilet paper. It's bad if they allow fraternizing a little too closely. We're still trying to figure out how to keep our dentists six feet away while they're poking around in our mouths.

"Obviously, we need to readjust to in-office meetings."

Coronavirus Lockdown – Phase Out 2

Dear Diary,

We think it's time to sign off for now. We're just going to hunker down and wait for a vaccine. Maybe we'll wait for the second or third wave of vaccines. We'll be a little on edge until the Gary Cooper of vaccines is created to obliterate COVID-19 at "High Noon." It's a good thing Howard Hughes was born too early to ever see this pandemic. It would have killed him.

As for all the people who think the pandemic is a hoax and refuse to wear masks, good luck to them.

Signing off,
Yin & Yang

Are you sure I'm Yang? I think I should be Yin.

I'm Yin. I will always be Yin. Stop yanging my yin!

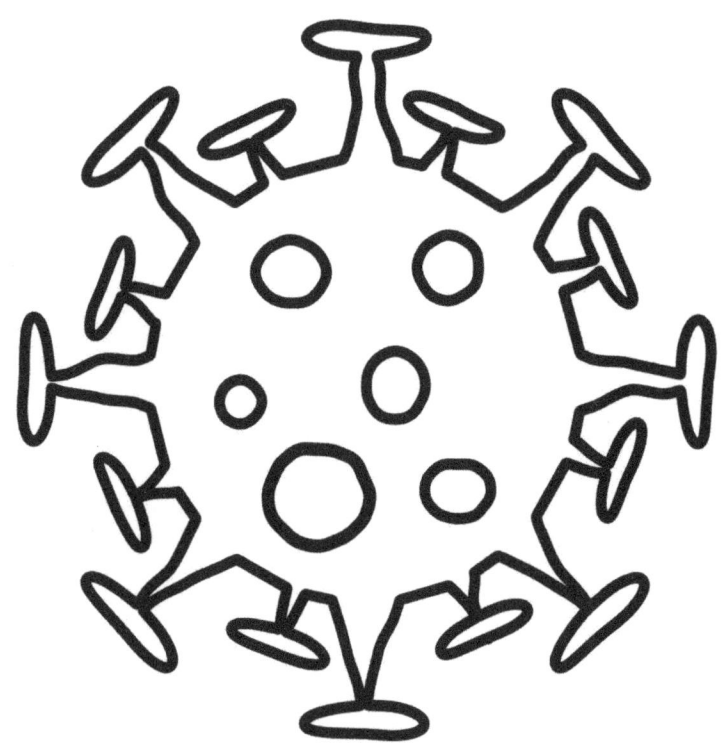

Milton Keynes UK
Ingram Content Group UK Ltd.
UKHW050405270124
436763UK00007B/157